Searching for Joy

Asha Godhia

BookLeaf Publishing

India | USA | UK

Presentation by *BookLeaf Publishing*

Web: www.bookleafpub.com

E-mail: info@bookleafpub.com

ISBN: 9789358317893

First edition 2023

I dedicate this book to those who have trouble getting started.

The hardest part is taking the first step.

"Start before you're ready. Don't prepare, begin."

- Mel Robbins

ACKNOWLEDGEMENT

It has been years since I last picked up a pen to write or read a book for pleasure. I started reading again a few years ago and created an Instagram page to share the books I was reading. Here, I connected with so many wonderful people, including other readers, authors, and writers.

A little thought began to form in my mind: what if I started writing again?

I recently started following and listening to Mel Robbins, who opened my eyes to the possibility of just doing. She stated, "If you want to sing, then sing; if you want to draw, draw; if you want to dance, dance. If you want to write, just start writing."

And that's how it happened.

Once I started writing, the words began to flow. The hardest part was setting aside the time to write, as there was always so much that I could and should have been doing. I think that's the problem with moms; we always find work to do.

I am grateful for the amazing inspiration that my dear friend Anita has given me. She started her own business, created a website and podcast from scratch, and even wrote a book! I am lucky to call her my friend. My sister Reena has also been my cheerleader, always believing in me and giving it to me straight. I know I can always count on her.

To my sweet husband, thank you for always standing by my side and holding me up when I needed it the most. Your never-ending support means the world to me, and I know that with you by my side, there's nothing that I cannot do. And to my sweet boys, the light of my life, thank you for bringing so much joy and love to my life and the world.

Always reach for the stars.

Xoxo,
Asha

Peace in our hearts

Two worlds colliding
An explosion of stars
Scattering across the sky
Little pockets of brightness
Lighting up the world

Death, despair, hatred
Clouding our vision, our sight
Poisoning our minds, our thoughts

Hostility stands in our way
Clouding our judgement
Holding us back, from what could be
Breaking down barriers
In our minds and in our thoughts
To making peace in our hearts.

My Son

From the sky to the ocean,
To the stars and the moon,
My love for you is like an ocean, vast and deep.

To watch you grow,
Standing tall and confident,
I know that you're becoming the kind of man
who can achieve anything he sets his mind to.

As you go through life,
Be true to yourself,
Hold fast to your values and beliefs.

Always listen to your heart and trust your
intuition,
So you can continue to grow and achieve your
dreams.

My Love

The twinkle in your eye
The smile playing upon your lips
The touch of your hand
The feel of your heartbeat
A gentle caress
A kiss
The warmth of your body next to mine
As I breathe you in,
Your love fills my soul.

A Summer's Day

A hot summer's day
Iced coffee in my hand

Wispy clouds float by
In the blue, blue sky

Birds chirping
Children's laughter fills the air

Peace
Comfort
Calm

I am home.

Nature Trails

Moss covered boulders sit upon the slopes
Branches stretching up, reaching for the sky
The sun peeks through the tall, tall trees

The air is crisp
The wind is cool
The sun is warm

The crunch of the leaves breaks through the
silence
The rush of the river fills the air
I look around

No other soul in sight
I breathe in the fresh air
I let it fill my lungs

And slowly, I breathe it out.

Hope

A little spark,
A glimmer of hope.
Sometimes that's all it takes.

Add in a breath,
A little bit of oxygen,
To get a fire going.

One word,
One action,
To cultivate a sense of trust.

A sense of community.
With shared values,
To have faith,
In each other.

That's okay to dream,
That it's okay to hope.
Because all we need is

That little spark.

Suffering

I suffer in silence as there's no one to hear the
screams
I'm surrounded yet no one takes notice

Do you see me?
Do you hear me?

Pain, sorrow, despair
Feelings, emotions all running rampant
Swirling, whirling, causing confusion and
disarray

I stand alone, looking out at the world
I reach out my hand and hope that it's not too
late.

My Wish for you

As shooting stars fly across the night sky,

My wish for you
To release the heartache from the past.
To acknowledge that it happened,
Blow a kiss and let the wind carry it away.

My wish for you
With every breath,
Release the tension in your heart.

Release the pain and hurt that has so tightly
wound itself
Like a vine wrapping itself around a tree,
Causing distrust and hesitation.

My wish for you
To open your heart
To help repair the damage to move forward.

Like a flower opening up,
Releasing its sweet fragrance
And sending it out into the world.

My wish for you
To choose love.

Grounded

I walk into the studio,
Barefoot and unsure.
I look around and see people greeting each other
Smiling and hugging, saying hello.

I find a spot in the corner and unroll my mat.
I feel the heat of the room,
My skin beginning to feel warm.
The scent of incense fills my nose,
As I take a deep breath and let it go.

I smile at my neighbor as I sit down,
Feeling a sense of calm wash over me.
Soft music fills my ears,
As I close my eyes and stretch out my body.

The mat beneath me is firm and supportive,
Like the ground beneath my feet.
I feel connected to the earth,
And to the people around me.

The instructor walks in and says
'Namaste, let's begin.'
And I know that I am exactly where I need to be.

Letting Go

Loud music fills my ear
My heart keeping pace with the rhythm.

Lights changing colour,
Reflecting off a disco ball hung on the ceiling.

Bodies of strangers, of friends moving in sync
Bumping into each other.

Arms up in the air
Faces bright, glistening with sweat.

Drinks are poured
Glasses are refilled.

I find myself surrounded
Hot, and sweaty.

Feeling the energy, as it flows through me
Pulsating, throbbing like a tremor.

The DJ changes the song
And the crowd goes wild.

I feel myself letting go
Letting the music wash over me.

Mirror

I look in the mirror,
I see my face staring back at me.
The tired eyes, the greasy hair
Falling limp across my shoulders.

The look of someone who's given up,
The light extinguished,
Feeling heavy
Weighted with grief, with pain.

Unable, unwilling to move forward
Heartache and heartbreak
Etched into the lines on my face.

No amount of makeup or lighting can erase
I see my tired eyes
And the truth of what lies within.

Seasons Change

As the seasons change from winter to spring,
I feel my mood rising,
Like seeds buried deep in the soil,
Slowly opening, roots beginning to emerge.

I am like a seed,
Being warmed by the sun's rays,
Cracking out of my shell,
Feeling lighter as the days go by.

Little by little, inch by inch,
As stems push through the soil,
I am finding myself again.

Finding my way back,
Letting myself be seen,
Not allowing myself to get pushed back into the
darkness.

I turn to face the sun,
Feel its warmth,
And absorb its light.

The light fills me up,
Like water filling a dry riverbed,

I am renewed.
I am a flower.

Opening up to the world,
Showing my true colors,
And letting my beauty shine.

A Photo

Stuck in a moment of time
No past no future

Just this moment
This feeling

Is it joy? Is it happiness?
Is it real?

Questioning thoughts
Questioning moments
Questioning time

To be out on the mantle, hung on the wall
Stored in a box deep in the attic
Collecting dust, cobwebs

Will anyone remember? Will anyone care?
For now, all that matters
Is this moment.

Autumn's Arrival

As a new month begins,
The air grows crisp and cool,
The days become shorter,
And the leaves start to fall.

It's a time for new beginnings,
A chance to start anew,
To set new goals and dreams,
And see them all come true.

The kids are back in school,
Creating new routines,
And as we turn the page,
We're ready to take on anything.

Like a brand new notebook,
Our minds are fresh and clear,
Ready to fill the pages,
With all we hold dear.

This season,
Full of endless possibilities,
Let's take on the challenge
And welcome Autumn's arrival.

Songbirds

Songbirds perched gracefully atop branches,
Singing their beautiful song,
Like an orchestra playing to the rhythm of the
wind.

Hidden by the thick abundance of green leaves,
Not seen by the passerby.

The sun's rays dance on the rippling water,
Warming it up for the birds to drink.

Once they've had their fill,
The birds take flight.

Their wings beating in perfect rhythm,
In search of another swaying branch,

To serenade us with their stunning song,
That echoes through the rustling leaves.

Invisible Chains

From the shadowy depths of the ocean
To the endless blue of a warm summer's day
The longing to be free never ceases to be
Invisible chains bind me
While the taste of freedom is just beyond reach

The choice to stay
The decision to go
A difficult proposition stands
Or is it?

Inspiration

Inspiration can be found wherever you look.
In the smallest moments and the grandest vistas.
It's in the single drop of rain,
Landing on a fallen leaf.
And in the branches dancing as the wind creates
waves through the leaves.

It's in the child's sudden laughter,
As their dog nuzzles their hand,
And in the tap tap tapping of a woodpecker,
As it searches for bugs to nourish its belly.

It's in the bright shining sun,
Reflecting off the glistening snow,
Sparkling like a field of diamonds.

All it takes is a moment,
Of quiet,
Of stillness,
To take notice,
Of the beauty that surrounds us all.

Rising to the Challenge

As the moon starts to rise and the darkness sets
in,
Another day is complete.
To start afresh,
The challenge of a new day.

From setting goals to writing lists,
What will you accomplish today?

The hours go by,
The world goes from dark to light.
The sun breaks out over the horizon.

It's scary to try something new,
Something you've never done before.
From trying a new recipe to rollerblading,
You hear the little voice that says, what if you
fail?

Take that risk,
Crack open that shell,
For this is how you grow,
This is how you learn to not be afraid,
To say, it's okay if I make a mistake.
I will try again.

Another day, another goal.
What will you accomplish today?

Sisters

Friendship, love, trust and acceptance
A connection of our hearts
Intertwining of souls
Bonds that cannot be broken
Some created by birth, others by choice
Open, honest, free of judgment

We fight, we cry, we hug, we laugh
No matter what life throws our way
We will always be, Sisters.

Freedom

I look in the mirror,
I see myself shrinking
Growing smaller and smaller
Until I am a small speck
And nothing more.

The wind picks up,
And I am blown away
Carried away into the skies
Into the clouds and over the horizon.

The wind carries me
Lifting me higher,
I am floating away
Over the trees, over the mountains.

The fresh air, the rejuvenating rain,
Enveloping me, releasing me.

I am free.

A Sea of Faces

Looking up at me
A sea of smiling faces,
full of love, joy, and innocence.
I am lost in the beauty of the moment.

To watch them learn and grow,
I am filled with wonder and amazement.
Their laughter and happiness
Precious and perfect.
A special gift just for us to care for and nurture.

My heart is full of love as I smile back at them,
With their beautiful eyes and smiling faces,
I am hopeful, I am grateful
I will cherish every moment.